DARING MISSIONS IN MATH

DEEP OCEAN DIVERS

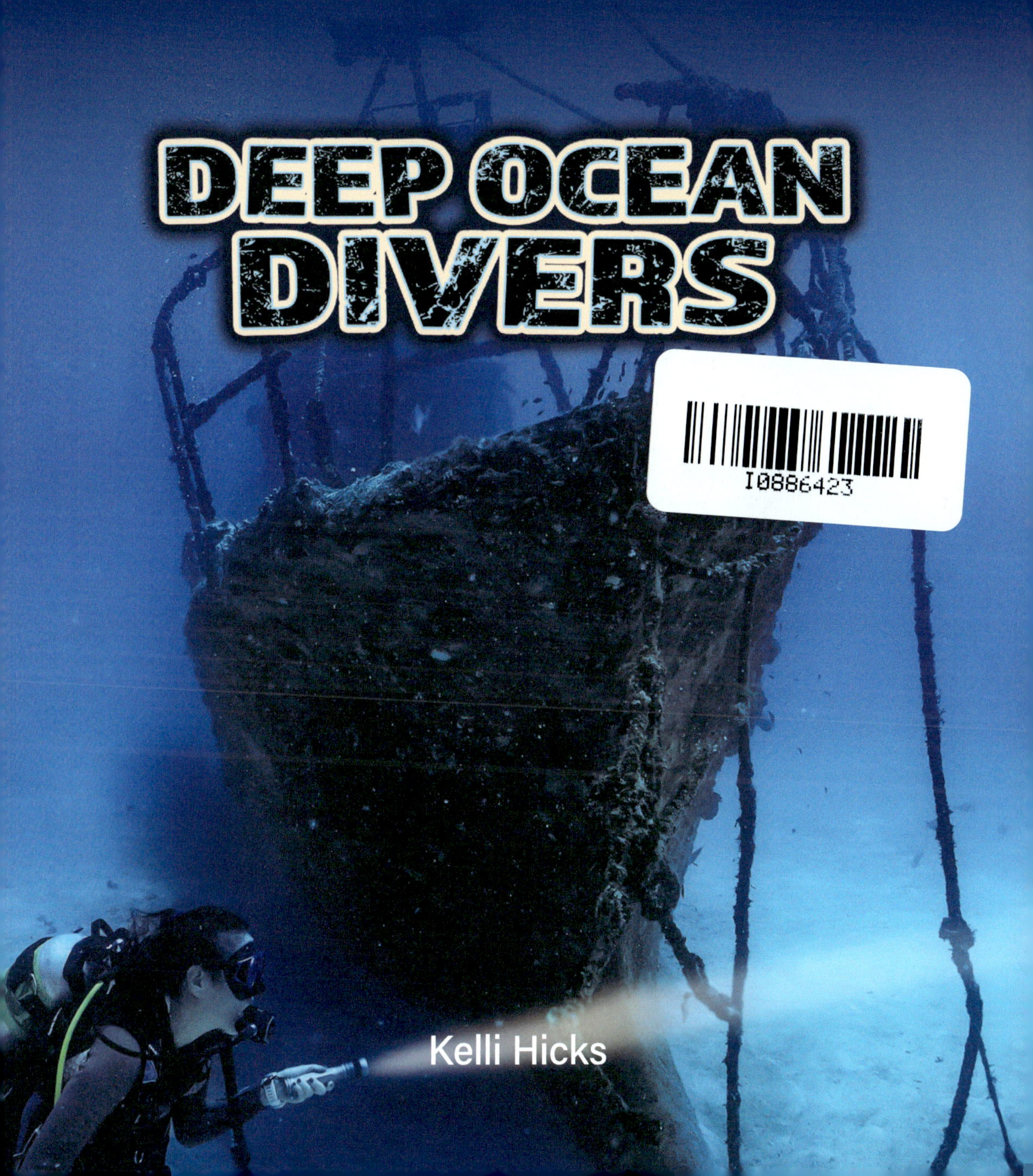

Kelli Hicks

Cherry Lake Press

Published in the United States of America by Cherry Lake Publishing Group

Ann Arbor, Michigan

www.cherrylakepublishing.com

Reading Adviser: Beth Walker Gambro, MS, Ed., Reading Consultant, Yorkville, IL

Photo Credits:
Cover © Sven Hansch/Shutterstock, (shipwreck and diver), © Evannovostro/Shutterstock, (sonar), © ranjith ravindran/Shutterstock, Folder graphic, (bottom right; Pg.4/5 ©ShuTunatura,ranjith ravindran,phmarcosborsatto. Pg.6/7 ©Nikolay Hristakiev/shutterstock, EmGIEF/Shutterstock, Drew McArthur/Shutterstock. Pg.8/9 ©Ann679/shutterstock.. Pg.10/11 ©Nyvlt-art/Shutterstock, JonMilnes/Shutterstock. Pg.12/13 ©TannerPhoto/Shutterstock, Lukas Gojda/Shutterstock, ukas Gojda/Shutterstock. Pg.14/15 ©Pixelsquid/shutterstock, Stefan Pircher/Shutterstock. Pg16/17 ©Nejat Semerci/Shutterstock, Pixelsquid/shutterstock. Pg18/19 ©agsaz/Shutterstock. Pg. 20/21©EmGIEF/Shutterstock. Pg22/23 ©Pixelsquid/shutterstock

Produced for Cherry Lake Publishing by bluedooreducation.com

Cherry Lake Press is an imprint of Cherry Lake Publishing.

Library of Congress Cataloging-in-Publication Data has been filed and is available at catalog.loc.gov.

Printed in the United States of America

Note from Publisher: Websites change regularly, and their future contents are outside of our control. Supervise children when conducting any recommended online searches for extended learning opportunities.

The content of this book focuses on measuring area, perimeter, and volume. Some metric conversions have been rounded to be grade-appropriate.

ABOUT THE AUTHOR

Kelli Hicks is a teacher, mom, and sports enthusiast who lives in Tampa, Florida. She loves learning about shipwrecks and the fascinating creatures that live under the sea.

TABLE OF CONTENTS

MISSION FILE

An unknown shipwreck has just been discovered. Dive into the investigation with a team of deep ocean divers.

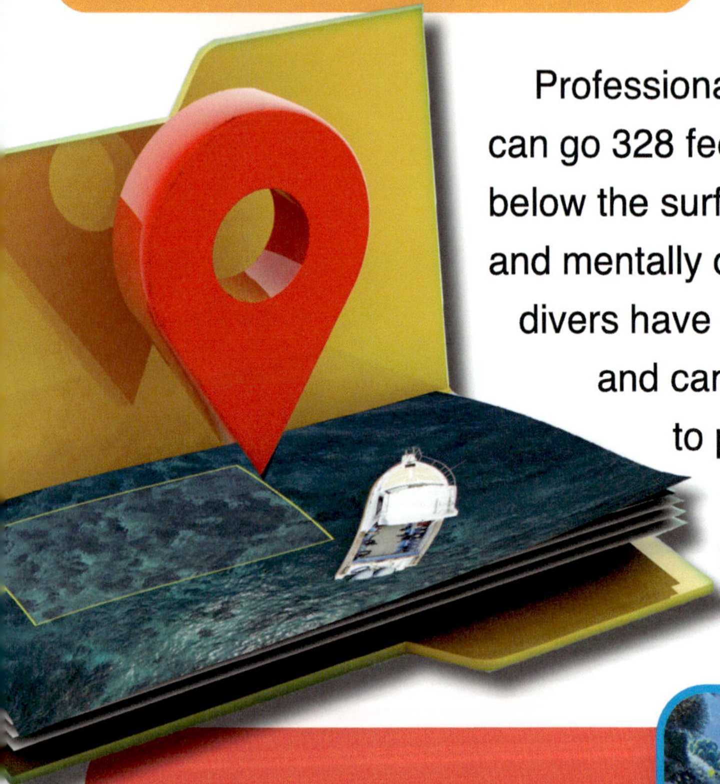

Professional deep ocean divers can go 328 feet (100 meters) or more below the surface. It can be physically and mentally difficult. Deep ocean divers have **extensive** training and can overcome dangers to perform jobs that no one else can. Will you measure up?

Many people **scuba** dive for fun. These kinds of divers need to have safety training and can only dive 130 ft (40 m) deep under water.

What special training is required to be a deep ocean diver? Once they have their scuba certification, deep ocean divers complete a course to learn about **decompression** and how to work at great depths for long periods of time. They train in a classroom, a pool, and the sea with an expert.

Our diving team consists of different types of deep ocean divers. Half of our divers are marine biologists. Half are underwater archeologists.

DIVER PROFILE

Marine Biologists

Marine biologists are scientific divers. They observe and interact with marine life. They dive to uncover information about changes in water temperature and how human interaction with the oceans are causing damage.

DIVER PROFILE

Underwater Archeologists

Underwater archeologists learn about the past by uncovering and studying **artifacts**. Some archeologists become dive experts to explore underwater lost cities or shipwrecks.

Deep ocean diving is dangerous! Because scuba divers breathe **compressed** air while underwater, pressure changes can cause lungs to over-expand if they surface too quickly. Divers may face aggressive marine animals or become trapped in a shipwreck or undersea cave.

MISSION PLAN

Before the mission begins, our boat captain will need the shipwreck's coordinates so that he can map a route. Let's locate the shipwreck on the map.

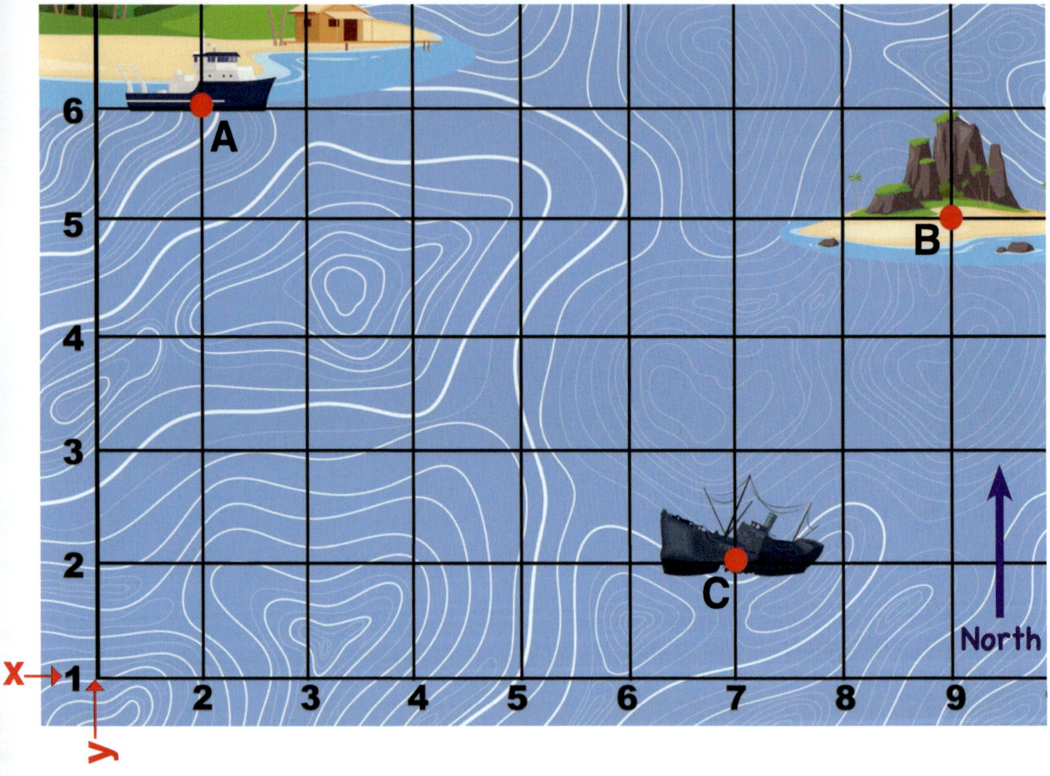

The *x*-axis represents the distance east and the *y*-axis represents the distance north. Our boat is furthest north at A (2,6). There is a small island at B (9,5). Where is the shipwreck (C) located?

The team needs to gather the diving gear and load it onto the boat. We have a cart to haul the scuba tanks. The **base** of the cart is 6 ft (1.83 m) long and 4 ft (1.22 m) wide.

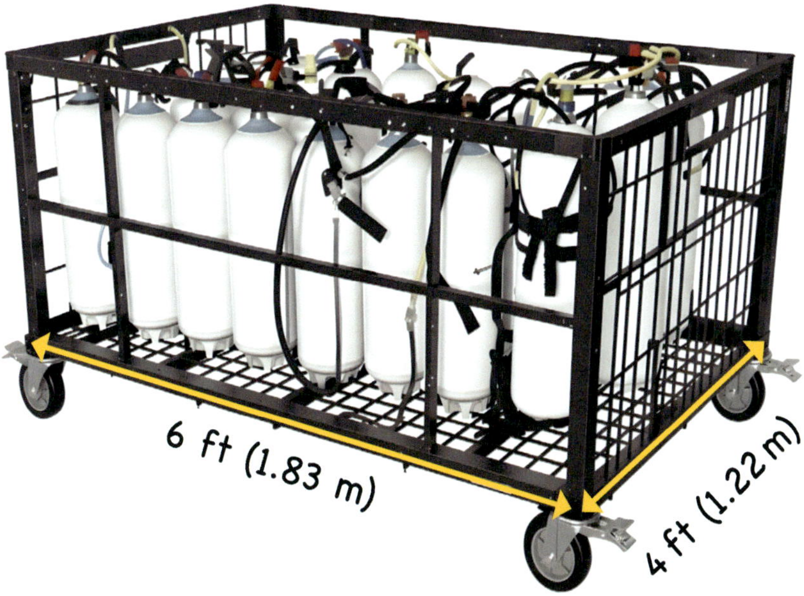

What is the area of the base of the cart?

Challenge Yourself!

On the boat, there is 35 square ft (3.25 square m) of space available for the cart. The space is 5 ft (1.52 m) wide. How long is it?

Think About It!

Area is the surface between given edges, measured in square units. To find the area, multiply the length times width:
6 ft x 4 ft = 24 square feet
(1.83 m x 1.22 m = 2.23 square meters)

Answer: The area of the cart's base is 24 square ft (2.23 square m).

To store the rest of our gear, we have 2 large storage boxes on the boat. Each storage box measures 3 ft (0.91 m) long, 2 ft (0.61 m) wide, and 4 ft (1.22 m) high.

What is the volume of each storage box?

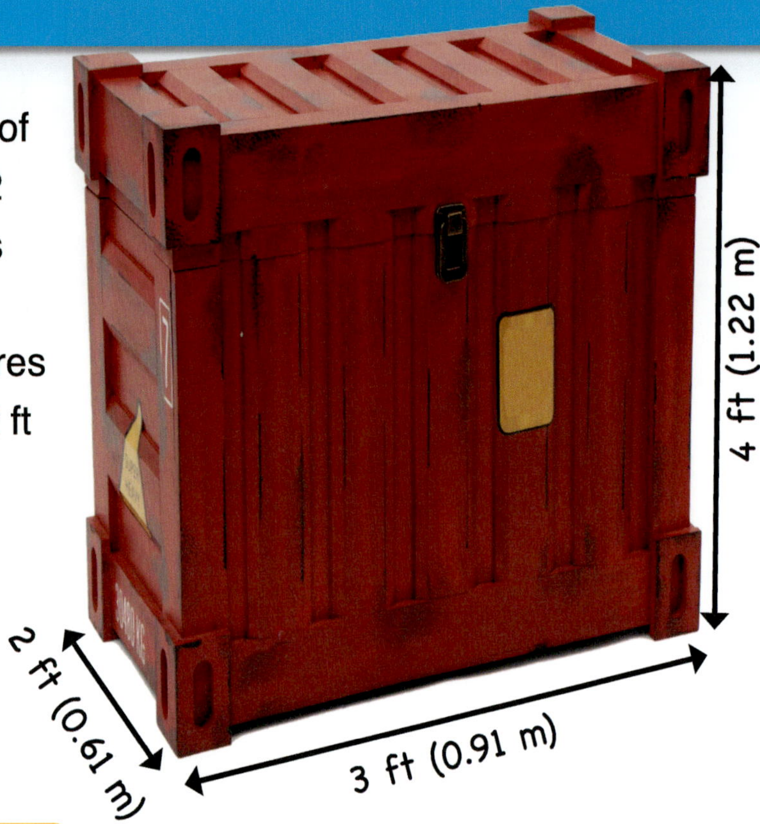

Think About It!

Volume is the amount of space taken up by a three-dimensional object. To find the volume of a square or rectangular box, measure length x width x height:

3 ft x 2 ft x 4 ft = 24 **cubic feet**
(0.91 m x 0.61 m x 1.22 m = 0.68 cubic meters)

Answer: The volume of one storage box is 24 cubic ft (0.68 cubic m).

How much space in volume do we have with 2 boxes?

Look at the lists below. How many sets of required gear can we fit into the 2 storage boxes?

If we take 6 sets of required gear, how many sets of optional items can we take?

REQUIRED GEAR SET
Volume: 6 cubic ft (0.17 cubic m)

- wetsuit
- fins
- mask and regulator
- buoyancy control device (BCD)

OPTIONAL ITEMS SET
Volume: 3 cubic ft (0.08 cubic m)

- underwater camera
- extra scuba tank
- waterproof flashlight

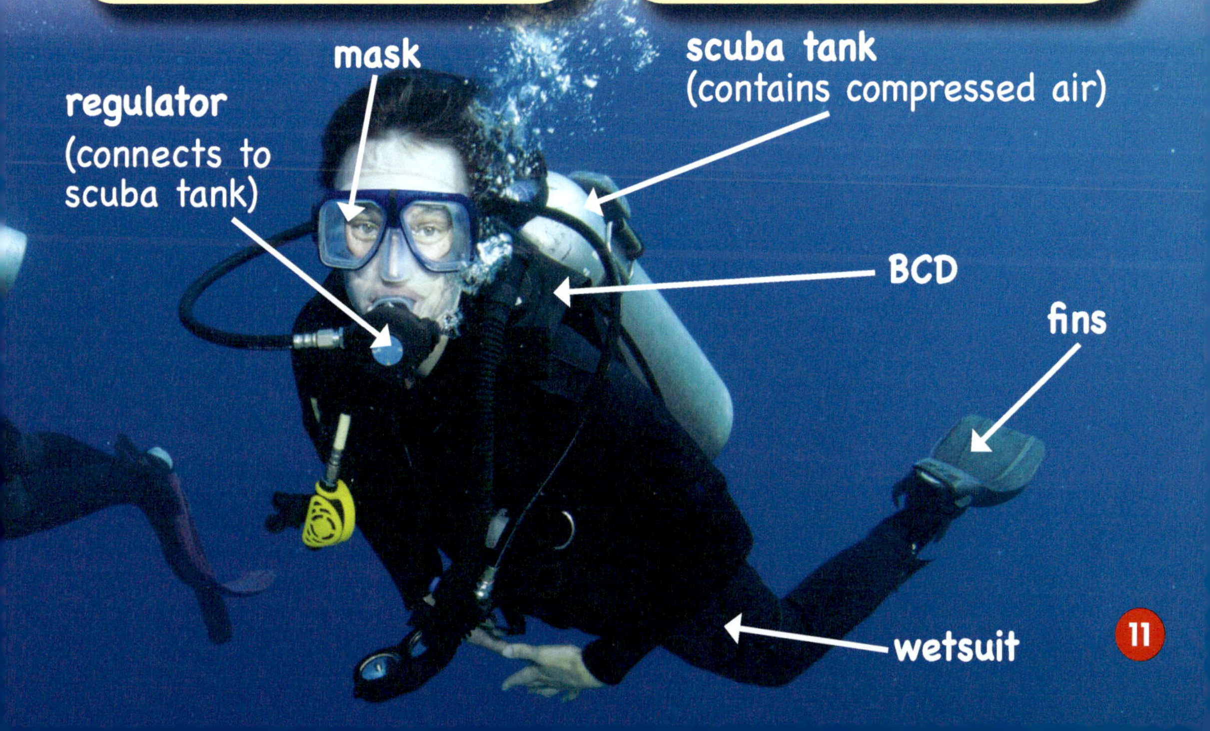

EXPLORING THE DEEP

The boat is ready with our gear on board and we head out to the site. A coral reef has grown up around the shipwreck. It lies 492 ft (150 m) deep. Two of our marine biologists put on their dive gear and make their **descent** first. They decide to map the coral reef and chart the animals found there.

They map a rectangular coral reef section that is 46 ft (14 m) long and 40 ft (12 m) wide. What is the total area of the coral reef section they mapped?

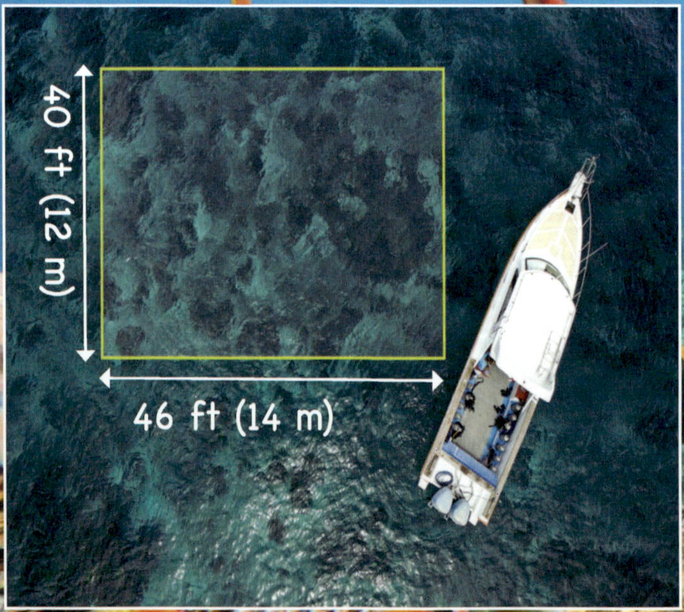

What is the perimeter of the coral reef section?

Challenge Yourself!

If each square meter contains about 3 coral species, how many coral species are estimated in the whole area?

Coral reefs are home to many animal species.

Think About It!

Perimeter is the distance around the edge of a shape, object, or place. To find the perimeter, add the length of all sides: 40 ft + 40 ft + 46 ft + 46 ft = 172 ft (12 m + 12 m + 14 m + 14 m = 52 m)

Answer: The perimeter of the coral reef section is 172 ft (52 m).

After the divers have successfully mapped the coral reef, our team gets a radio message that there have been shark sightings nearby. The safest way to dive with sharks is in cages. Luckily, we have one on board.

The rectangular dive cage has a length of 14 ft (4.27 m). The total perimeter is 38 ft (11.58 m). What is the width of the cage?

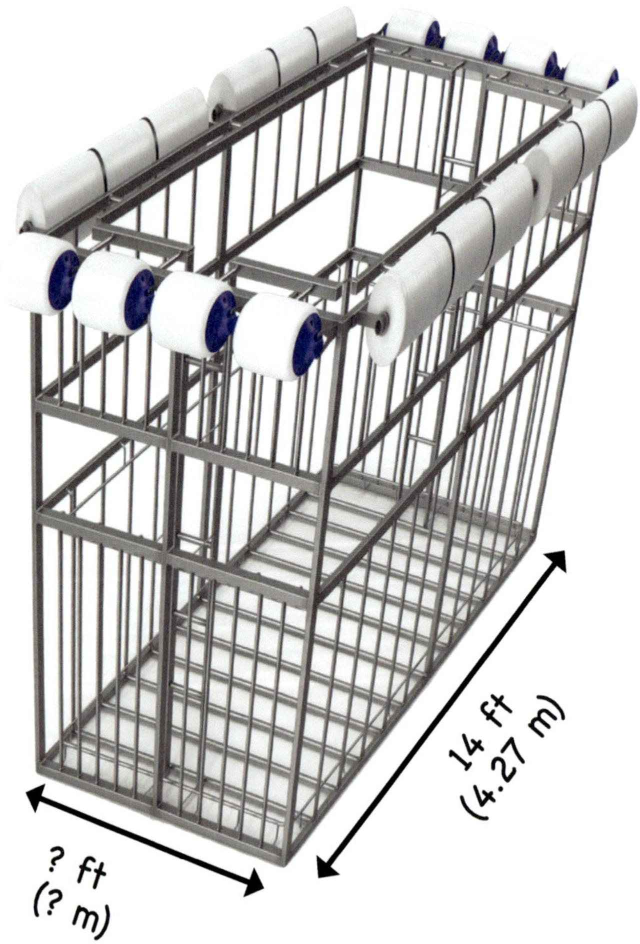

Steel or aluminum make the cage strong. The vertical bars are close enough to prevent sharks from entering or biting into the cage.

DIVING INTO HISTORY

We begin putting on our dive gear. We get another radio message telling us that the sharks are now 10 miles (16.0 kilometers) away. We decide not to use the shark cage and go into the ocean.

Before exploring, we need to map the site. We section off two connected rectangular sections.

The first section is 39 ft (11.89 m) long and 13 ft (3.96 m) wide. The second section is 26 ft (7.92 m) long and 13 ft (3.96 m) wide. What is the total area of the site?

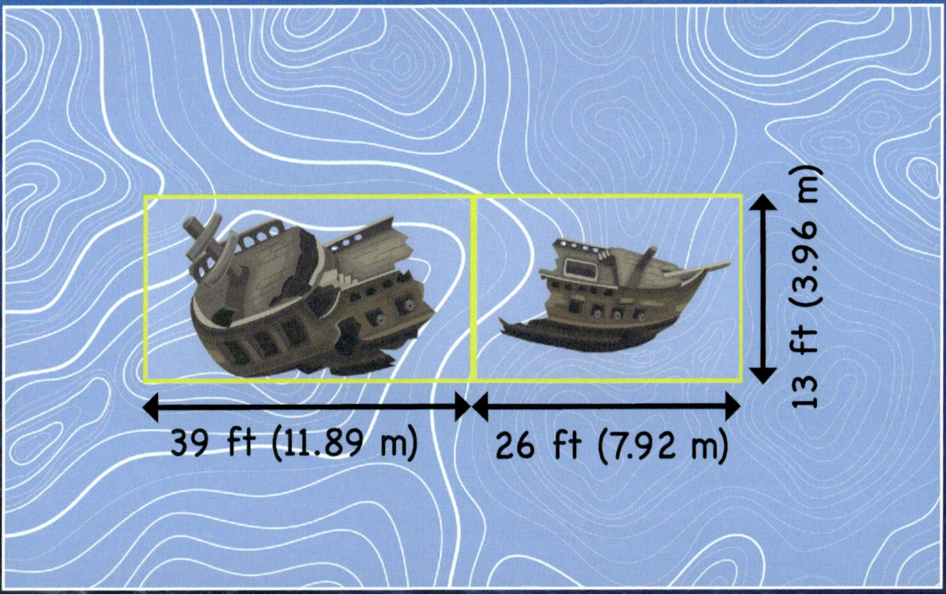

Shipwrecks can tells us a lot about history, including how people lived.

The archeologists on the team **estimate** the ship sank around 300 years ago. Parts of the inside of the boat are covered in sand. The sand helped to preserve the **cargo** on the boat. We want to find out what is in the cargo hold.

The cargo hold is 12 ft (3.66 m) long, 12 ft (3.66 m) wide, and 10 ft (3.04 m) high. What is the volume of the cargo hold?

The cargo hold in old ships can be found in the lower decks. This provided the most amount of space to transport crates, barrels, and other cargo.

Inside the cargo hold we find barrels and 15 wooden boxes. We are excited to know what's inside them.

The 15 wooden boxes are all the same size. Altogether, they take up 960 cubic ft (27 cubic m) of space. Using the information below, what is in the 15 boxes? Did we find treasure?

One box of cloth measures:
600 cubic ft (17 cubic m).

One box of tools measures:
96 cubic ft (2.72 cubic m).

One box of dishes measures:
64 cubic ft (1.80 cubic m).

One box of treasure measures:
30 cubic ft (0.85 cubic m).

MISSION ACCOMPLISHED!

Despite the possible threat of sharks, our brave team gathered valuable information about the ship and the reef. Our training, the right equipment, and teamwork made our mission a success.

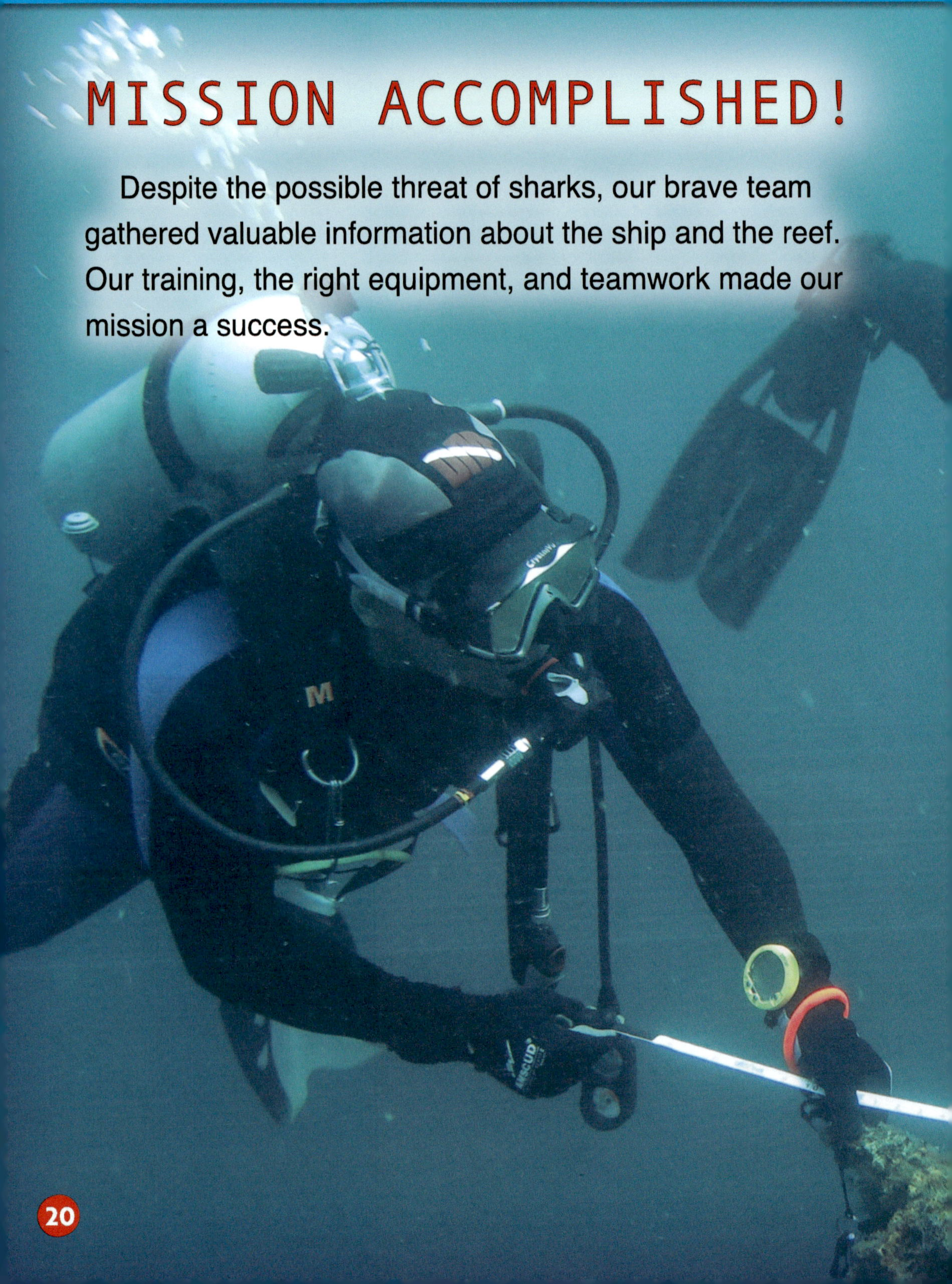

Wreckage from over 250,000 sunken vessels litter the world's oceans. They include pirate ships loaded with treasure, as well as modern warships and submarines. Most of them lay undiscovered.

Answers

Page 8: Using points on the coordinate plane, we can identify different locations on the grid. To find a location on a coordinate plane, move across the *x*-axis first. Then, move up or down to find the point on the *y*-axis. Always note the *x*-axis number first. **Answer:** The shipwreck is located at (7,2).

Page 9: To find out how long the space is, we can divide the area by the width. 35÷5=7 (3.25÷1.52=2.14). **Answer:** The length of the space is 7 ft (2.14 m). Let's check! 5x7=35. (1.52x2.14=3.25)

Page 10: If each storage box volume is 24 cubic ft (0.68 cubic m), multiply by 2 to find the total volume of both boxes. **Answer:** The total volume of both boxes is 48 cubic ft (1.36 cubic m).

Page 11: To find out how many sets of required gear we can fit into 2 storage boxes, divide the volume of both storage boxes by the volume of 1 set of required gear:
48 cubic ft÷6 cubic ft=8 (1.36 cubic m÷0.17 cubic m=8).
Answer: We can fit 8 sets.

To find out how many sets of optional items we can fit if we take 6 sets of required gear, first subtract the volume of 6 sets of required gear from the storage boxes' volume:
6 sets of required gear: 6x6=36 cubic ft. 6x0.17=1.02 cubic m
48 cubic ft−36 cubic ft=12 cubic ft (1.36 cubic m−1.02 cubic m=0.34 m).
Divide the remaining volume by the volume of 1 set of optional items:
12 cubic ft÷3 cubic ft = 4. (0.34 cubic m÷0.08 cubic m = 4.25). **Answer:** We can take 4 sets of optional items.

Page 12: To find the area, multiply the length times the width. **Answer:** The area of the coral reef section is 46 ft x 40 ft = 1840 square ft (14 m x 12 m = 168 square m).

Page 13: To find the total number of species, multiply the square meters by the number of species.168x3=504 **Answer:** There are about 504 species of coral.

Page 14: To find the perimeter, we add all sides. If the length of one side is 14 ft (4.27 m), then the opposite side is also 14 ft (4.27 m). Add both sides and we get 28 ft (8.54 m). Take this total away from the perimeter 38 ft−28 ft=10 ft (11.58 m−8.54 m=3.04 m). The total of the last two sides are 10 ft (3.04 m). That means each side is 5 ft wide (1.52 m). **Answer:** The width of the cage is 5 ft (1.52 m).

Page 17: To find the area, multiply the length times the width of each section:
39 ft (11.89 m) x 13 ft (3.96 m) = 507 square ft (47.08 square m).
26 ft (7.92 m) x 13 ft (3.96 m) = 338 square ft (31.36 square m).

Add the two sections' areas to find the total area.
507 square ft (47.08 square m)+338 square ft (31.36 square m)=845 square ft (78.44 square m). **Answer:** The total area of the site is 845 square ft (78.44 square m).

Page 18: To find the volume of the cargo hold multiply its length times the width times the height: 12 ft (3.66 m) x 12 ft (3.66 m) x 10 ft (3.04 m) =1,440 cubic ft (40.72 cubic m). **Answer:** The cargo hold's volume is 1,440 cubic ft (40.72 cubic m).

Page 19: We know that the 15 boxes take up 960 cubic ft (27 cubic m) of space. To find the correct box, divide 960 cubic ft (27 cubic m) by 15. 960÷15=64. (27÷15=1.8). **Answer:** 64 cubic ft (1.80 cubic m). The boxes are full of dishes.

Test Yourself

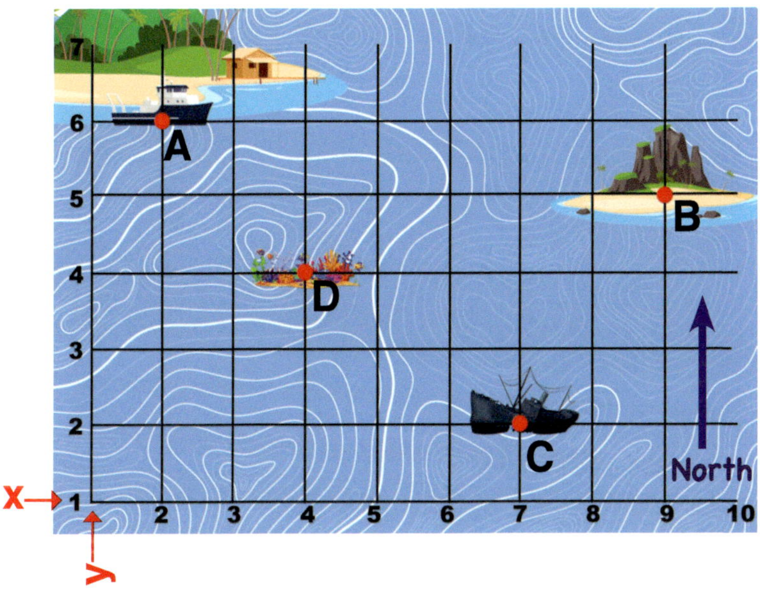

1. What are the coordinates for the coral reef (D)?
2. What is the total area of a sunken ship if the length of the ship is 20 ft (6.0 m) and the width is 9 ft (2.74 m)?
3. What is the volume of a crate if the length is 10 ft (3.04 m), the width is 10 ft (3.04 m), and the height is 4 ft (1.22 m)?
4. A cargo hold is 12 ft (3.66 m) long. The perimeter is 48 ft (14.64 m). How wide is the cargo hold?
5. The volume of a container on the ship is 30 cubic ft (0.84 cubic m). We know the length is 5 ft (1.52 m) and the width is 3 ft (0.91 m). What is the height of the container?

Answers: 1. (4,4) **2.** 180 square ft (16.44 square m) **3.** 400 cubic ft (11.27 cubic m) **4.** 12 ft (3.66 m) **5.** 2 ft (0.61 m)

Find Out More

Books

Adler, David A. *Perimeter, Area, and Volume: A Monster Book of Dimensions*. New York, NY: Holiday House, 2012.

O'Daly, Ann. *Measuring Area*. New York, NY: Powerkids Press, 2023.

Websites

Search these online sources with an adult:

Coordinate Planes | IXL Learning

Intro to Area and Perimeter | Khan Academy

Glossary

artifacts (AR-tuh-fakts) objects made by human beings in the past

base (BAYS) the lowest part of something

buoyancy control device (BOY-uhn-see kuhn-TROHL dih-VIES) an inflatable vest that helps divers control their buoyancy and depth in water while diving

cargo (KAR-goh) goods that are carried by a ship or aircraft

compressed (kuhm-PREST) pressed or squeezed to fit in a small space

cubic feet (KYOO-bik FEET) a unit of measurement used for volume

decompression (dee-kuhm-PRESH-uhn) a reduction of air pressure

descent (dih-SENT) go down to a lower level

estimate (ES-tuh-muht) make a rough guess or calculation

extensive (ek-STEN-siv) includes or covers a great many things or very large area

scuba (SKOO-buh) a word shortened from **s**elf-**c**ontained **u**nderwater **b**reathing **a**pparatus

Index